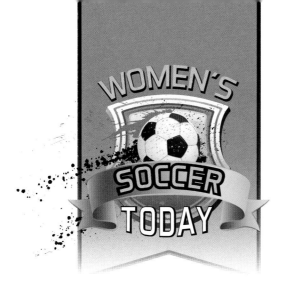

# SUPERSTARS OF WOMEN'S SOCCER

# WOMEN'S SOCCER TODAY

WOMEN'S SOCCER TODAY

# SUPERSTARS
## OF WOMEN'S
# SOCCER

BRYCE KANE

MASON CREST

Mason Crest
450 Parkway Drive, Suite D
Broomall, Pennsylvania 19008
(866) MCP-BOOK (toll free)



First printing
9 8 7 6 5 4 3 2 1

ISBN (hardback) 978-1-4222-4213-1
ISBN (series) 978-1-4222-4212-4
ISBN (ebook) 978-1-4222-7595-5

Library of Congress Cataloging-in-Publication Data on file

Developed and Produced by National Highlights Inc.
Editor: Andrew Luke
Interior and cover design: Annalisa Gumbrecht, Studio Gumbrecht
Production: Michelle Luke

## QR CODES AND LINKS TO THIRD-PARTY CONTENT

# CONTENTS

## KEY ICONS TO LOOK FOR:

 **WORDS TO UNDERSTAND:** These words with their easy-to-understand definitions will increase the reader's understanding of the text while building vocabulary skills.

 **SIDEBARS:** This boxed material within the main text allows readers to build knowledge, gain insights, explore possibilities, and broaden their perspectives by weaving together additional information to provide realistic and holistic perspectives.

 **EDUCATIONAL VIDEOS:** Readers can view videos by scanning our QR codes, providing them with additional educational content to supplement the text. Examples include news coverage, moments in history, speeches, iconic sports moments, and much more!

 **TEXT-DEPENDENT QUESTIONS:** These questions send the reader back to the text for more careful attention to the evidence presented there.

 **RESEARCH PROJECTS:** Readers are pointed toward areas of further inquiry connected to each chapter. Suggestions are provided for projects that encourage deeper research and analysis.

## WORDS TO UNDERSTAND

**dynamic**
pertaining to or characterized by energy or effective action; vigorously active or forceful; energetic

**intuitive**
based on what one feels to be true even without conscious reasoning; instinctive

**superlative**
the highest quality or degree

**tactical**
of, relating to, or used for a specific plan that is created to achieve a particular goal

6

# CHAPTER 1

# Who's Number One?

Women's soccer is a **dynamic** sport that has changed rapidly over the years. While many of the top players remain the same for years, new and younger stars are always on the rise. Currently, four women stand apart as the top female soccer players in the world. These four footballers are Lieke Martens, Pernille Harder, Wendie Renard, and Lucy Bronze. Each of these athletes has many accomplishments that place her at or near the top of this list.

# 2017 FEMALE PLAYER OF THE YEAR

Among her many accomplishments as a soccer player, Dutch midfielder/ forward Lieke Martens was named the Best FIFA Women's Player of 2017 at the FIFA Gala. FIFA (Fédération Internationale de Football Association) is the sport's international governing body, and the gala is an annual event at which it announces each year's award winners across the sport. Martens won this award after winning the Women's Euro, or the UEFA (Union of European Football Associations) Women's Championship for the Netherlands over the summer of 2017. Martens is likely to make a big splash in the 2019 FIFA Women's World Cup in France and help the Netherlands compete at a **superlative** level.

Martens was born on December 16, 1992, in Bergen, which is a city located in the Limburg province of the Netherlands. Martens enjoyed soccer from a young age. She joined Dutch club teams SC Heerenveen from 2009 to 2010 and VVV-Venlo from 2010 to 2011. The following season Martens played at Standard Liège in the Belgian First Division, which is the top women's soccer league in Belgium.

*After eight seasons playing in Holland, Belgium, Germany and Sweden, Martens now plays for the famous FC Barcelona in Spain.*

Martens's international career reached an early peak in the 2010 UEFA European Women's Under-19 Championship. It was during this competition that she scored four goals to tie Turid Knaak as the top scorer for the event. It was also this championship that really turned people on to Martens, who became an international women's soccer celebrity overnight. Her fun, friendly, and humble interviews have become very popular on YouTube and other video sites. In 2011, she played in a friendly against China for her first match on the Netherlands's senior national team.

Her skills as a player inspired Dutch coach Roger Reijners to select her for the 2015 FIFA Women's World Cup squad. Martens did not let Reijners down, as she became the first player to score a Women's World Cup goal in Dutch team history during that tournament. Later on, she scored three goals in the Netherlands's 2017 UEFA Women's Euro campaign. Other titles she has helped her teams win over the years include the 2011 BeNe Super Cup, the Svenska Cupen in 2015–2016, the Svenska Supercupen in 2016, and the Copa de la Reina de Fútbol in 2018.

*After Martens joined the team, Barcelona won its league championship by a whopping 14-point margin.*

The most prominent example of Martens' playing excellence came during her debut season with FC Barcelona in 2017. The club had been increasing its success over the previous few years before adding Martens's, but she helped to take them over the top. Just how much did they improve over that time?

With Martens's help, her squad won their first four games by a shocking goal differential of 23–0. That is just under a 6–0 scoring average and was, by far, the best differential in the league during that period. Barcelona ended the season as the top team in La Liga with ninety-three points, scoring ninety-nine goals versus twenty-nine scored against them. They won twenty-eight games, drew nine, and lost just one. Their closest competitor, Atlético Madrid, had only seventy-nine points and fifty-eight goals scored on twenty-two scored against with a record of 38–5–10.

## PLAYING STYLE

Martens is a midfielder and forward known to play an aggressive style of soccer that focuses on quick dribbles and scoring off the pass. Coach Stefan Rehn compared her style and technique with that of Manon Melis. Melis is one of the top Dutch female soccer players of all time and is the all-time leading scorer for her country. Like Melis, Martens has a clear understanding of the soccer field and the ways that soccer plays develop.

One of her signature moves is a quick header for a stunning goal. There are many highlights of her taking a cross from a teammate and getting it into the back of the net using just her head. However, she is also known as a skilled **tactical** thinker who works hard to not only get into scoring position but also to help her teammates by separating from defenders to take a pass for a goal.

## A Typical Training Routine for Lieke Martens

Training takes up a lot of Martens' schedule and leaves her little time to relax between significant competitions. For example, she is known to work heavily on creating strong, stable, explosive legs. Her routine centers around a basic step-up paired with weights. The weights increase the intensity of the routine and improve its effectiveness. Other training routines she uses include the side step-up and kick, as well as a suitcase deadlift and lateral step-up. Each of these exercises is performed during a multi-hour daily training session that also includes cardiovascular training. Soccer players don't get a lot of time to relax if they want to be the best in the world.

*Martens was named FIFA Best Women's Player in 2017.*

# PERNILLE HARDER: ALSO THE BEST?

In 2017, striker Pernille Harder of Denmark won the first-ever female version of the Goal 50 award for being the best player of the season. Goal.com is a UK-based soccer website that is the second-largest online sports publication in the world. Being named top player by Goal.com is a less-prestigious honor than winning FIFA Best Player, but it shows that some experts think Harder is better than Martens. Harder was also the runner-up in the UEFA Women's Player of the Year Award in 2016–2017, losing out to Martens. Ironically, Martens defeated Harder in the 2017 UEFA Women's Euro tournament, which is likely why she, and not Harder, won the award.

Harder, who like Martens is just twenty-six, debuted on the Denmark national team in 2009 at the age of seventeen. Since then, she has made a major impact on the international soccer community. She has been the captain of the team since 2016 and helped lead them to the UEFA Women's Euro championship game in 2017, a game in which she scored a goal. Before this experience, she was probably best known for her time with Linköpings FC, the Swedish club where she scored seventy goals in just eighty-seven matches from 2012 to 2016.

At the 2008 FIFA Under-17 Women's World Cup, sixteen-year-old Harder scored a hat trick in a stunning 15–0 win over Georgia. Hat tricks have become something of a trademark for Harder, as she scored them against Austria and Armenia in 2011 and another against Russia in 2013.

*Harder's long hair flows behind her as she streaks down the field dribbling the ball during a UEFA Women's Champions league match in 2018.*

She was Denmark's top qualifying scorer in the 2013 Women's Euro with nine goals. And while Germany ultimately went on to win the championship in that competition, Harder's efforts helped make Denmark one of the top qualifiers and a team to watch out for in the 2019 Women's World Cup tournament.

# PLAYING STYLE

Like Martens, Harder is known for an aggressive and upbeat playing style. This method matches the typical Denmark approach, which is to keep moving, pass frequently, and score goals on quick-developing plays. This high-tempo style of soccer has become ideal for many clubs around the world. It contrasts with the slower and more tactical play that is common with more traditional clubs, such as Germany.

Here are a few shocking statistics that showcase just how good Harder has become. In her first eight years of senior club play, she scored 115 goals with seventeen coming in domestic cup matches. During the same time, she scored more than fifty goals for Denmark's national team. And her international cup career, which started in 2014, has earned her eight goals. For those keeping score at home, that's upward of 160 goals in seven years. To put that into perspective, that's an average of more than twenty-twos goals every year.

*Watch Pernille Harder lead Denmark past Poland in the 2017 Euro.*

## Wendie Renard,
## Center Back
### *(France/Lyon)*

✓ Only player voted to the first three FIFPro Women's World XI Teams (2015, 2016, 2017)

✓ 2015 FIFA Women's World Cup All-Star

✓ **MORE THAN 100 CAPS**

## Lieke Martens, Midfielder
### *(Netherlands/Barcelona)*

✓ **2017 BEST FIFA WOMEN'S PLAYER**

✓ 2017 UEFA Women's Player of the Year

✓ Golden Ball winner, 2017 Women's Euro

# WORLD CLASS SUPERSTARS

## Lucy Bronze, Defender
### (England/Lyon)

- Two-time PFA Women's Players' Player of the Year (2014, 2017)

- FA WSLS 1 Players' Player of the Year (2016)

- **BBC WOMEN'S FOOTBALLER OF THE YEAR (2018)**

## Pernille Harder, Striker (Denmark/VfL Wolfsburg)

- **THREE-TIME DANISH FOOTBALL PLAYER OF THE YEAR (2015, 2016, 2017)**

- Frauen-Bundesliga top scorer (2018)

- 2018 UEFA Women's Player of the Year

# A HIGH STANDARD

Wendie Renard is a defender on the French women's soccer team who is likely to make a significant impact on the Women's World Cup in 2019. This center back defender was born in Martinique in 1990 and moved to mainland France later in her life to join Olympique Lyon. She continues to play with this club and has helped lead them to five consecutive league titles between 2006 and 2011. With her help, Lyon was also able to win the Challenge de France (called the Coupe de France Féminine since 2012) in 2008, and then in six consecutive years from 2012 to 2017.

One of her most significant moments on the international scene came in 2010 when Renard and Lyon competed in the UEFA Women's Champions League. This competition pits the best club teams from all across Europe against each other to determine the best of the best. In the 2010–2011 competition, Renard was one of the most critical players for her team. Her intelligence and skills helped lead the team to the championship game against Turbine Potsdam. After she scored the first goal, her team scored another to blank Turbine 2–0 for the win.

*Renard leads her Olympique Lyonnais teammates during a warm-up lap prior to the UEFA Women's Champions League final in 2018.*

During her career at Lyon, she has scored forty-seven league goals through 2018. However, she has also scored eleven cup goals, making her one of Lyon's best scorers during this period. In 2013, her presence on the French soccer scene was impressive enough to help her get named to the previous two Women's World Cup and Olympic teams for France. She has been the captain of both of these crews since 2013. Their successes in these competitions has inspired a whole new generation of female soccer players to emulate Renard's tough, dedicated, and unforgettable playing style.

# PLAYING STYLE

Renard is known as a great two-way player who can both score and play defense with ease. She and her teammates have created a brand of soccer that focuses on skillful team interaction and an intuitive understanding of the way games develop and change. Defense is a particularly critical part of the French approach with Renard.

*Renard (3) slides to the ground as she scores the opening goal during the 2011 UEFA Women's champions league final.*

Unlike many other defenders, Renard is also feared as a potent scoring threat. She has scored nineteen goals during her career on the French national team. One of her biggest accomplishments was being the only player nominated for the first three editions (2015 to 2017) of the Women's World XI, an international all-star team selected by the players themselves.

# TOUGH AND HONEST

Lucy Bronze is an English soccer player who has become one of the best defenders in the world. So far, she has won the Professional Footballer's Association (PFA) Women's Player of the Year Award twice. The PFA is the player's trade union. The first win came in 2014 and the second in 2017. As a result, many experts say that she'll be an important part of England's run-up to the FIFA Women's World Cup in 2019.

Bronze's career has been an interesting one because she has played for both French and English clubs. She currently performs with Olympique Lyon in France as a club player but competes for England in World Cup and Olympic tournaments. Her primary position is right back, and she is a defensive anchor for any team that she joins.

Interestingly, she played college soccer briefly in the United States at the Division I level. In fact, she was the first British soccer player ever to win an NCAA soccer championship after she helped lead the North Carolina Tar Heels to a national title in 2009.

After this championship season, she moved on to join English clubs Sunderland Woman, Everton, Liverpool, and Manchester City. With these clubs, she made an immediate impression on English soccer and has become one of the most watched players in the country.

Bronze's career began at the youth level in England, where she was one of its most promising players. In the 2007–2008 season, she was named

*Bronze is a two-time winner of the PFA Women's Player of the Year.*

Manager's Player of the Year as her team finished third in its division. In 2009, she competed in the FA Women's Cup final, and though Sunderland lost 2–1 to Arsenal, Bronze was named the player of the match.

Bronze was the defensive lynchpin in England's successful run to third place at the 2015 FIFA Women's World Cup. In fact, many experts are confident that Bronze's team will be one of the most interesting teams to watch in the 2019 tournament. Some are even picking them as a dark horse candidate for a championship run.

## PLAYING STYLE

Bronze is a defense-oriented player who can shift to offense in the blink of an eye. This adaptability makes her a tough player to compete against because she is unpredictable. One moment she is shutting down a play with a high-quality tackle and the next she is scoring a goal on a header.

While Bronze doesn't have the goal count of her French counterpart Renard, she is critical to England's defensive efforts. She focuses on doing all of the little things right, such as skillful dribbling, precise passing, and powerful shooting. This diverse range of abilities makes her a dangerous player on any team. For example, her seventy-sixth-minute goal against Norway in the 2015 FIFA Women's World Cup was the game-winner that lifted England out of the round of sixteen and into the quarterfinal, where they beat Canada 2–1 en route to a third-place finish in the tournament.

# TEXT-DEPENDENT QUESTIONS:

**1.** Who was the first female winner of the Goal 50 award for the best footballer on the planet in 2017?

**2.** In what year was Lieke Martens the top scorer at the U-19 Euro with four goals?

**3.** At which American university did Lucy Bronze play?

# RESEARCH PROJECT:

How do organizations like FIFA rank their female soccer players? Research the statistics and playing information that they use to rank their players. Create a chart that showcases this information, and highlight how this decision-making process has changed over the years. Include statistics, when possible, to support your points.

# WORDS TO UNDERSTAND

**dark horse**
a candidate or competitor that is not expected to succeed but has the potential to achieve a surprise result

**linchpin**
a person or thing vital to an enterprise or organization

**meticulously**
showing great attention to detail

**tenacity**
the quality of being very determined; persistence

# CHAPTER 2

# Super Strikers

Strikers are often the linchpins of any successful soccer team. They are responsible not only for scoring a majority of a team's goals but also must help their teammates get into scoring positions. At every moment in a game, a good striker must be thinking of ways to put the ball into the back of the net, leaving the goalie stunned.

# ADA HEGERBERG

When it comes to women strikers who are likely to stun the world during the 2019 FIFA Women's World Cup, Ada Hegerberg of Norway is one of the best. Even though she is just twenty-four years old, Hegerberg has already made a significant impact on the sport as a striker. In fact, her presence on Team Norway could make them a dark horse candidate that ends up surprising the experts.

*Hegerberg is the youngest player ever to score a hat trick in Norway's top women's league, the Toppserien.*

## GREATEST SUCCESSES

Soccer is something of a family affair for Ada, as she grew up playing youth soccer for Sunndal Fotball club with her older sister Andrine. In fact, Andrine is a skilled midfielder who will be playing alongside her sister at the 2019 FIFA Women's World Cup. Both women are very respected players in their country and on the international scene.

After debuting for senior club Kolbotn in 2010 (at the age of fifteen), Ada Hegerberg and her sister made a huge splash the following year in a match against Røa. Ada scored three goals in just seven minutes with big sister Andrine adding one as well to finish a flurry of scoring that stunned their opponent 4–1. In fact, at only sixteen years old, Ada was the youngest player to score a hat trick in Toppserien, the top-level women's league in Norway.

In that same 2011 season, Hegerberg was voted the league's Young Player of the Year and finished as the league's top scorer with twelve goals. Her success as a striker and her chemistry with Andrine helped both players join Stabaek in 2012. Ada did not disappoint the team, as she was the top scorer with twenty-four goals in just eighteen games.

In 2012 Hegerberg scored five goals in the semifinal and final games of the Norwegian Women's Cup to lead her team to 3–0 and 4–0 wins over Amazon Grimstad and Røa, respectively. Both she and her sister signed with FFC Turbine Potsdam in Germany in 2013 and then with Olympique Lyonnais in 2014. It was with this team that she scored twenty-six goals in twenty-two league games to lead them to a ninth-consecutive Division 1 Féminine title in 2014. With Hegerberg leading the league in goals scored with thirty-three, Lyon won three titles the following season—a tenth-straight league title, the Coupe de France national title, and the UEFA Champions League title.

*Hegerberg works on her ball control during warm-up for the 2018 UEFA Women's Champions League Final in the Ukraine.*

# GREATEST SKILLS

Professional soccer scouts have defined Hegerberg's playing style as goal centric and adaptable. She succeeds in many types of playing styles and formations, excelling in the attacking 4–2–3–1 formation in particular. Her strengths are defined primarily by her ability to spot scoring opportunities and her sharp and accurate shots.

Scouts say the biggest weakness she displays is a relative lack of strength as a passer. While she is by no means a mediocre passer, accuracy issues have been noticed during a few match situations. That said, Hegerberg is also known to be an expert dribbler who particularly excels in tough one-on-one situations.

In spite of potential weak spots in her game, Hegerberg is one of the most skilled and promising strikers in the sport. She has essential international soccer experience, as she played on the 2015 UEFA Women's Championship squad and was also on the 2015 FIFA Women's World Cup team for Norway.

In the 2015 World Cup, she scored three goals in the group stage matches to help Norway tie with Germany in Group B with seven points. This result was good enough to get them to the round of sixteen, where they lost a tight 2–1 match against England. With four more years of experience under her belt, there's a good chance Hegerberg could help push Norway even further in 2019.

# Yes, Soccer Does Include Set Plays

The average person watching his or her first soccer game may think that it is based all on reacting to the moment and using superior speed to outflank an opponent. However, that is only one part of the sport. Set plays are often designed for situations such as kickoffs, free kicks, corner kicks, and throw-ins. During these situations, players create unique formations designed to allow scoring chances or prevent them. Set plays can be used to either attack the goal directly with a shot or to get the ball into scoring position for teammates. However, players are also taught to take specific positions and formations during the flow of the game to improve their chances of scoring on the fly.

# SAMANTHA KERR

*Australia's Sam Kerr is one of the most prolific goal scorers in the women's game. She is the leading career goal scorer in the NWSL.*

Ever since the beginning of the FIFA Women's World Cup tournament, the Australian team has been improving its game. While it did not qualify in 1991, it has qualified for every tournament since then. And starting in 2007, the team has clawed its way out of the group stage in every competition. Since then, the Australian team has reached the quarterfinals in every competition, but has never finished higher than sixth.

However, Aussie luck could change in 2019 if Sam Kerr has anything to do with it. This striker is one of the most dominant players in the world and could be the spark plug her country's team needs to power it towards higher success. Her diverse playing career has been filled with plenty of success already, and capping it off with a World Cup Championship would be the next big step.

# A LATE START

Unlike other strikers in this chapter, Kerr is a relative newcomer to soccer. In fact, she didn't start playing until she was twelve years old, having played Australian Rules Football before making the switch. She started playing youth soccer with the Perth-based Western Knights from 2006 to 2008 before beginning her senior career with Perth Glory FC of the Australia W-League at the age of fifteen from 2008 to 2011.

By that time, dedication and constant practice had helped Kerr become a dominant player. In fact, she was awarded Goal of the Year for an incredible long shot against Sydney FC and was voted Player's Player in round eight of the 2009 W-League playoffs. Her success in this women's league tournament included three goals in ten games and a brace in the first half against Adelaide United in 2011 to help secure the 2–1 win for Perth.

*Kerr started her pro career with the Perth Glory in Australia's W-League.*

Her speed and athleticism made her a desirable option for many clubs around the world. After being courted by many teams, Kerr left home and signed with the Western New York Flash of the National Women's Soccer League (NWSL) for the 2013 season. During her twenty-one appearances for the club (nineteen of which were starts), she scored six goals and led the Flash all the way to the finals before losing 2–0 to Portland. During this time, her head coach Aaran Lines said, "if she continues to develop at the rate she is, Sam can become one of the best strikers in the world."

After a successful 2014 season with the team (during which she scored nine goals), she was traded to New Jersey's Sky Blue FC. Though she has since played on other professional teams, her breakout moment was likely a match during her NWSL 2017 season. During this match against Seattle, Sky Blue FC was down 3–0 at halftime. Kerr dominated with four goals in the second half to help Sky Blue win 5–4. In that season, she won the NWSL Golden Boot and MVP awards and finished with seventeen goals, a single-season record. Kerr is the leading goal scorer in the NWSL's short history.

# "I WANT TO BE CRISTIANO RONALDO"

This quote, attributed to Kerr in 2017, says a lot about her playing style. Ronaldo, the five-time FIFA World Player of the Year, is renowned as one of the most recognizable faces in men's soccer and is known for an offensive-minded and aggressive style of play, including eight goals in four World Cup tournaments. With her similar combination of speed and tenacity, Kerr is known to attack the goal at every opportunity, no matter what the game situation. Her four-goal effort to spark the comeback win against Seattle in that 2017 NWSL match is an excellent example of her refusal to give up. Like Ronaldo, Kerr is an aggressive player who strikes at the goal often. She is also an expert passer and

*Kerr hurdles a Canadian defender in pursuit of the ball during a match at the 2016 Olympic games.*

dribbler who rarely gives up the ball. That tenacity and drive could help her lead Australia to its first-ever FIFA Women's World Cup final match appearance ever in 2019.

In fact, Kerr has already made a significant impact on the national team by scoring the game-tying goal in a match against Japan in 2018 to secure the team a spot in the 2019 World Cup. If they had lost this game to the Japanese team, their chances of qualifying would have been much lower. Appropriately enough, this goal came against the same Japanese crew that eliminated Australia from the 2015 World Cup.

*Watch Sam Kerr score four goals in a dramatic come-from-behind win.*

Kerr's desire to play like Ronaldo showcases her dedication and drive toward being the best player in the world. Unlike more extroverted players, Kerr tends to keep quiet and let her success on the field do the talking for her. But don't let her quiet nature fool you. On the pitch her game speaks volumes, and she's a dangerous player that is likely to do a lot of damage to her opponents at the 2019 FIFA Women's World Cup.

# ALEX MORGAN

When most Americans think of women's soccer, they are likely to think of Alex Morgan. This striker has been one of the most dominant players in the sport for years, and at twenty-nine she is one of the most decorated strikers in the game. Not only is she a national champion in Women's Professional Soccer (WPS), but she is also a FIFA Women's World Cup champion and an Olympic gold medalist.

In fact, she is one of the primary reasons that the United States has maintained a dominant edge in the sport. While the team has won three championships since the debut of the FIFA Women's World Cup in 1991, the addition of players like Morgan has helped keep the USWNT prominent over the last two decades and into the foreseeable future.

# FORESEEABLE SUCCESS

Morgan's professional career began when she was drafted at number one in the 2011 WPS Draft by the Western New York Flash. This draft pick came after she graduated early from the University of California, Berkeley and was a breakthrough moment for the young player. In fact, she helped the Flash win a championship that year.

*Morgan poses on the red carpet at the 2018 ESPY awards as she attended in support of several teammates nominated for awards.*

After that debut season, she decided to jump to the Seattle Sounders Women team for the 2012 season, stating at the time that she was excited to play in a city that enjoyed women's soccer. The Sounders were one of the most popular teams in the league and had attendance rates four times higher than any other. Unfortunately, Morgan was able to make only three appearances during the regular season due to her preparation for the 2012 Summer Olympics.

Since that season, Morgan has also played for the Portland Thorns and Orlando Pride of the NWSL. She helped lead Portland to the first NWSL Championship in 2013. Unfortunately, the success of the Thorns waned over the next three years, as they were eliminated from the playoffs two years in a row and failed to qualify in 2015. As a result, Morgan joined the Pride in 2016.

# INTERNATIONAL STARDOM

Morgan's first World Cup appearance came in 2011 when the USWNT finished second. She was just twenty-two at the time and was the youngest player on the team. In spite of her youth, she was a pivotal player to the U.S. team's success in that World Cup. In 2012, she became only the second American woman to score at least twenty goals and twenty assists in the same year, with twenty-eight goals and twenty-one assists. The only other player to hit these marks is Mia Hamm.

Despite the fact that Morgan was recovering from a knee injury before the 2015 Women's World Cup, she was added to the team before the tournament and started in every game. As a result, she led the team to a 5–2 win over Japan to win the team's third World Cup Championship. She only scored one goal during

*Morgan is one of only two female American players ever to score at least twenty international goals and twenty assists in the same year.*

the competition, but she did hit a few shoot-out penalty kicks and played a crucial part in controlling the action on the field.

# MORGAN MAY BE THE MESSI OF FEMALE SOCCER

Like Lionel Messi, Morgan is one of the most recognized players in her sport and one of the most respected. Messi is an Argentinian soccer superstar who is a five-time FIFA World Player of the Year and the winner of the FIFA World Cup Golden Ball award in 2014.

While other players may score more goals than these two, both Morgan and Messi possess very high soccer IQ levels. Both can read the flow of the soccer field and open up scoring possibilities by setting up successful plays.

And like Messi, Morgan's style is focused on **meticulously** creating the best potential scoring possibilities, rather than sending an endless barrage of shots at the goal. That style quirk doesn't mean that either isn't capable of scoring based on raw strength and speed. Like Messi, Morgan is one of the fastest and most reliable players in the league and capable of raw-power shots that blow past the defending goalie.

*Morgan played the 2017 European season with French team Lyon.*

Beyond her play on the pitch, Morgan is an author and has also become known as a philanthropist and a great role model for young female soccer players. Her series of young adult books, *The Kicks*, is filled with inspiring stories about overcoming tough odds and achieving success. And her fight for gender income equality brought up an important point: though far more successful than the men's national team, the U.S. Women's National Team does not get the same level of pay.

# VIVIANNE MIEDEMA

The Netherlands is likely to be an exciting team to watch at the FIFA Women's World Cup because of its striker Vivianne Miedema. This player is one of the most promising and skilled strikers in the world. When she made her debut at age fifteen, she was the youngest player in the Eredivisie Vrouwen league in the Netherlands. During her 2013–2014 season for Heerenveen, she scored an astonishing thirty-nine goals, easily making her the top scorer for her league.

Other early successes for Miedema came in the 2014–2015 season playing for Bayern Munich in Germany. During this season, she and her young team went unbeaten in the league and won the team its first title since 1976. In the 2014 UEFA Women's Under-19 Championship tournament, she scored six goals and led her team to the title. She was awarded the Golden Player title as the best player in the tournament.

# THE NETHERLANDS'S FIRST WORLD CUP APPEARANCE

The Netherlands's women's team had struggled to make a dent in the international sport until Miedema joined in 2014. In fact, during a playoff match against Italy in 2014 her efforts helped the team qualify for its first-ever FIFA Women's World Cup appearance in 2015. During this tough match, Miedema made her presence known immediately by scoring a hat trick and leading her team to a 3–2 win.

Miedema was the top scorer for the qualification games, scoring sixteen goals and propelling her team into international tournament play. At the time, Miedema was just eighteen years old and was one of the youngest players to compete in a qualifying game. In fact, many publications and professionals were already proclaiming her to be the best striker in all of Europe.

During the Netherlands's 2015 World Cup campaign, the Dutch team came in third in Group A with four points, tying with China PR and trailing Canada by just one point. They were then eliminated from the round of sixteen in a tight 2–1 game against Japan. Since then, Miedema has shown signs of only getting better with age.

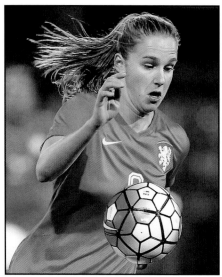

*In just four years Miedema rocketed to second place on the all-time women's goal-scoring list for the Netherlands.*

For example, Miedema was the primary factor in the Netherlands's 2017 UEFA Women's European Championship win. Her winning goal in the semifinal against England helped push them to the final game against Denmark. Miedema's two goals in the final helped propel the team to a 4–2 win and were good enough to make her the second-best scorer in the championship with four total goals.

Her mature personality and her high level of intellect have partially inspired Miedema's success on the field. Though just twenty-three, her teammates regularly praise her wisdom, her on- and off-field focus, and her multilayered understanding of the game. That maturity is likely to deepen as Miedema progresses as a player and will help her turn into one of the most successful players of her generation.

# TWO-FOOTED PLAYING STYLE

Miedema (or Viv as her teammates know her) is one of the most precise and powerful strikers in the sport. However, she does not succeed on just raw strength. Like other strikers, she has practiced scoring from multiple angles and in various positions and has built up the muscle memory needed to take the best shot in the right situation.

Miedema is also known for playing a two-footed style. This ambidextrous approach means that she can dribble, pass, and shoot from either side. As a result, she has a diverse array of possible shooting options.

*Miedema is dangerous on the rush because she has the skill to strike with equal ability with either foot.*

# TEXT DEPENDENT QUESTIONS:

**1.** How many goals did Samantha Kerr score in a 5–4 come-from-behind victory in 2017?

**2.** Which striker plays alongside her older sister on the national team?

**3.** Who has been called "The Female Lionel Messi"?

# RESEARCH PROJECT:

Research the physics and geometry concepts behind scoring a goal. Map out the best possible angles for a striker to score and recreate them on graphing paper. Now watch a few soccer matches and see how often players get into these positions during a game.

 WORDS TO UNDERSTAND

**acclaim**
strong approval or praise

**blank**
to keep an opponent from scoring

**unprecedented**
never done or known before

# Midfield Mavens

Strikers own the faces that you primarily see endorsing the most products or adorning magazine covers. After all, they provide that rare and valuable commodity of the sport—the goals. Experts will say, however, that midfield is where the match is controlled, not upfront. Not only do midfielders control possession and the tempo, but they can set up the attack as well.

*During her three seasons in Houston from 2015 to 2017, Lloyd scored eleven goals in just twenty-seven appearances for the Dash. Her time with her club team was interrupted by obligations to the USWNT for the 2015 World Cup and 2016 Olympics.*

# CARLI LLOYD

Midfielders may not get as much attention as strikers, but as American Carli Lloyd has shown, they can be just as deadly when it comes to scoring. Lloyd started playing soccer when she was only five, back when the teams were coed. As a result, she learned how to play rough against the hard-hitting boys. While attending Delran High School in New Jersey, she performed as a midfielder and was known for her ball control and ability to get the ball into scoring position from the middle of the field.

During her senior year she was a fixture as a midfielder and Delran's captain who scored twenty-six goals and eight assists en route to an 18–3 record. Recruited by Rutgers University to play for the Scarlet Knights, she was named First-Team All-Big East for four years. She was the first Rutgers athlete ever to earn this honor. When she finished her college career, she was the school's all-time leader in goals with fifty.

# MOVING ON TO CLUB AND PRO BALL

While in high school, Lloyd started playing for W-League teams including the Central Jersey Splash, New Brunswick Power, and South Jersey Banshees. Later on, she continued playing for these teams during the NCAA off-season. With the debut of Women's Professional Soccer (WPS) in 2009, Lloyd started playing professionally for the first time in her career.

Her time in the WPS started with the Chicago Red Stars. In spite of her strong defensive skills and her ability to score from midfield, she scored only two goals as the Red Stars finished 5–10–5 on the season. After becoming a free agent, she signed with Sky Blue FC for 2010. Her debut with her home-state team, unfortunately, ended early when she broke her ankle.

After recovering from this injury, she signed with the Atlanta Beat for 2011 and continued to show high-quality playing skills. Unfortunately for her, the team was ill-prepared for the season and finished in last place with a 1–13–4 record.

# FINALLY, SOME PROFESSIONAL SUCCESS

Playing on mediocre teams that struggled to score against higher-quality opponents had plagued Lloyd's professional career up to 2013. However, her skills and adherence to a team-oriented mindset were rewarded when she signed with the Western New York Flash in the National Women's Soccer League (NWSL). One of her best moments during this season was scoring a hat trick against the Washington Spirit to win 4–0.

Surrounded by a skilled crew, Lloyd excelled and scored ten goals to finish third on the NWSL goal-leaders list. The Spirit's 10–4–8 record helped them advance to the playoffs, where Lloyd's two goals in the

*Lloyd started playing for the USWNT in 2005 at age twenty-three.*

*Watch some highlights of Carli Lloyd's 2017 season.*

semifinals advanced the Flash to the finals, which they lost 2–0. In 2015, Lloyd was traded to the Houston Dash for two years and then back to Sky Blue FC in 2018.

Perhaps because her success came a little later in life and after some tough personal trials, Lloyd has remained surprisingly down-to-earth. She has kept her life clean and orderly and avoided controversy despite the national attention she receives. In fact, she is married to her high school sweetheart and is known to still visit her local New Jersey beauty shop for occasional manicures and pedicures.

# TWO WORLD CUP TOURNAMENTS

In 2011, Lloyd was chosen for the World Cup squad, which was her debut experience on the sport's biggest stage. She came out strong by scoring the final goal in a 3–0 win against Colombia. This was her first-ever World Cup goal. She earned another goal, got an assist, and hit a penalty kick against Brazil to send her team to the semis. Unfortunately, after reaching the final match, Lloyd and two other teammates were unable to convert penalty kicks in the shootout following a 2–2 full time result against Japan, which led to a loss that earned the USWNT second place.

Her success in the 2011 tournament and her professional **acclaim** made Lloyd one of the highest-profile athletes at the 2015 World Cup. Scoring quickly and often throughout the tournament, she scored six total goals to help her team win the championship. Her most significant moment came in the final rematch against Japan, during which she scored a hat trick in the first sixteen minutes. Her hard work earned her the nod for the Golden Ball as the best player of the tournament. Expect similar results in 2019.

# MARTA

In sports there is no bigger type of acclaim than being known by a single name. Players like Shaq and LeBron in basketball are known beyond the sport and are identifiable worldwide. In Brazilian men's soccer, there are a few such one-name athletes: Pelé, Ronaldo, Romário, and Neymar. For the women, there is only Marta.

*Brazilian superstar Marta won five consecutive FIFA Women's Player of the Year awards from2006 to 2010.*

Like Pelé, Marta is often considered the best player in her sport. Born and raised in the tiny western Brazil town of Dois Riachos, she was discovered at the tender age of fourteen and started her professional career for Vasco da Gama, a popular club in the big city of Rio de Janeiro. From there, she made the jump to Europe at eighteen and joined Umeå IK in Sweden, a country in which she would eventually earn dual citizenship with her native Brazil.

*At the club level, Marta played eleven seasons in Sweden, a country where she is also a citizen, most recently for FC Rosengård from 2014 to 2017.*

# A STORIED CAREER

In spite of being primarily a traditional number ten, an attacking midfielder, Marta scores at a striker-level rate. She has played all of the attacking positions throughout her career. For example, in the 2004 UEFA Women's Cup final she helped Umeå IK win against Frankfurt 8–0 on aggregate with three goals scored. That year, the team scored a league-leading 106 goals, 22 of which belonged to Marta. In fact, she scored the only goal in the 2–1 loss against Djurgården in the Swedish cup final, one of the few losses the team suffered that year. Individually, Marta's brilliance as a teenage phenom was acknowledged when she was voted third for FIFA World Player of the Year. Her second season was a similar success, with the team sweeping the league and Marta scoring twenty-one goals, finishing second in the Player of the Year voting.

Shockingly, Umeå IK lost 3–1 in the 2005 Swedish cup final to Djurgarden, in spite of crushing them 7–0 just a few weeks prior. The next year, she contributed another twenty-one goals in an undefeated season but again lost the national championship, 3–2. This time, however, she won the FIFA World Player of the Year award for the first of a record five-straight years. In 2007, history repeated itself with the team losing 1–0 in the Swedish cup final.

After the 2008 season Marta, who was at the time clearly the best female player in the world, made the massive announcement that she would be moving to Los Angeles to play for the Los Angeles Sol of the WPS. During that time, she was the league's top scorer with ten goals and three assists. The Sol, with Marta's help, moved on to the WPS Championship final but fell 1–0 against Sky Blue FC. She later played briefly with Santos FC, FC Gold Pride, and the Western New York Flash. Marta finished in the top three for FIFA World Player of the Year in eleven-straight seasons from 2004 to 2014.

# WOMEN'S WORLD CUP CAREER

Marta's first Women's World Cup appearance was in 2007 for Brazil. During the group stage, she contributed four goals to help Brazil move easily to the knockout rounds. In the quarterfinals, she helped the team win 3–2 against Australia with a penalty-shot goal. In the semifinal round, she scored twice to help Brazil blank the U.S. 4–0. However, Germany then blanked Brazil 2–0 in the final, though Marta won the Golden Ball as the top player and the Golden Boot as the top scorer with seven goals.

In 2011, Brazil once again strolled easily through the group stages but was eliminated by the United States in the quarterfinals. Marta's four goals and two assists moved her atop the Women's World Cup all-time scoring list, tied with German legend Birgit Prinz. At that point, both players had scored fourteen goals in combined World Cups. Her hard work earned her the Silver Boot as the second-leading scorer.

In 2015, she scored against South Korea to take the lead on the Women's World Cup all-time scoring list with fifteen goals. In this tournament, Brazil advanced easily to the knockout stage by winning all three games and outscoring their opponents with a 4:0 goal differential. Unfortunately for them, Australia came out strong in this round and knocked Brazil out of the tournament with a 1–0 win.

# WHY MARTA IS SO GOOD

Marta's **unprecedented** scoring success has a lot to do with her quick feet and her skill with the ball. Marta is one of the fastest dribblers in the game and capable of easily maneuvering around other players. Her passing skills are also strong, which is key to her success as a midfielder. However, her technical skills are also considered among the highest.

For example, her cross passes and penalty kicks showcase a technical understanding of the sport that is similar to that of Pelé and other championship players. One of her trademarks is the penalty kick, and she is known to practice scoring from this position for hours before a tournament begins.

Like Alex Morgan, Marta is an advocate for better pay for female soccer players. She has stated that the sometimes unstable world of the female soccer player can be unsettling, as many are never sure if they'll have a team to play for the next season. And in spite of her accolades, she is known for her humble personality and her distaste for talking about herself and her success. In that way, she resembles Pelé even more.

*Marta is the all-time leading scorer in the history of the FIFA Women's World Cup with fifteen goals.*

# World Cup Celebrations Are Wild

Soccer fans take the World Cup very seriously. Every four years, people gather together in homes, restaurants, and other viewing areas to watch their home nations compete. Every goal their teams score causes an immediate eruption of excitement. However, every goal scored against them is a painful experience that is hard to handle. And when a team wins, the thrill of the moment can get rather wild. In 2015, American fans were thrilled when the women's team cruised to an easy 5–2 championship victory over Japan, which was made even sweeter as it served as revenge for the 2011 final loss against the same team. When they won, the celebrations lasted for days and included parades and all-night parties.

# DZSENIFER MAROZSÁN

There is no end to the qualifications of Germany's Women's World Cup team. They have two championships to their name and have made three other deep runs into the tournament. Germany has finished in the top four in five of the seven FIFA Women's World Cups. In 2015, they placed fourth after being eliminated by the United States. However, a young player named Dzsenifer Marozsán may be the key addition that pushes them to increased success in the 2019 FIFA Women's World Cup.

This nationalized German citizen has soccer loyalty in her family, as her father János Marozsán was a four-time Hungarian football national star. After moving to Germany at a young age to advance her soccer career, Marozsán quickly made a significant impact on the sport—one that is still being felt today.

*Marozsán battles two defenders for the ball while playing for Lyon in the 2018 UEFA Women's Champions league final.*

# STARTING YOUNG

This midfielder was signed to play in the Frauen-Bundesliga (Germany's top women's league) at the age of fourteen years and seven months, making her the youngest player ever in the league. While playing for FC Saarbrücken, Marozsán also set a record as the youngest goal scorer in the league when she dropped one in the back of the net at the age of fifteen years and four months. During her time with this group, she scored thirteen goals and secured a German Cup runner-up placement in the 2007–2008 season.

Since then, her career has seen a lot of ups and a few downs. She signed with FFC Frankfurt from 2009 to 2016 and appeared in 133 matches while scoring forty goals. That kind of goal-to-match ratio is incredible for a midfielder in any day and age. The fact that she did it in the highly competitive top German league is all the more impressive. During this time, her team was a runner-up in the 2011–2012 UEFA Women's Champions League and the winner in 2014–2015.

## JOINING LYON

In 2016, Marozsán signed with Lyon in France and made an immediate impact. In the 2016–2017 season, Lyon was the winner of the Division 1 Féminine, the UEFA Women's Champions League, and the Coupe de France Féminine.

## INTERNATIONAL CAREER

For Germany, she helped win the UEFA Women's U-17 Championship in 2008 and the FIFA U-20 Women's World Cup in 2010. In 2010 she debuted with the senior team and was eventually a big part of the team's UEFA Women's Championship in 2013.

After helping the German national team get a fourth-place finish in the 2015 World Cup, Marozsán made a big international splash at the 2016 Rio Olympic Games when she blasted home the winning goal in a 2–1 win over Sweden in the final match. This gave Germany its first-ever women's soccer Olympic gold medal. After the Olympics, the German team named Marozsán captain.

*Marozsán debuted with the German senior national team in 2010.*

# WHAT TO EXPECT FROM MAROZSÁN

Anyone who has watched her play knows that they can expect an exciting and prodigious experience from Marozsán. She is an attacking midfielder but is skilled at both offense and defense. One of her signature moves is the full-field pass to a striker patiently waiting at or near the net.

Like any good midfielder, Marozsán has an instinctive grasp of the flow of the game on the field. Unfortunately, this leads to some people criticizing her for lacking initiative—for example, in some situations she may pass to a teammate instead of taking what seems to be an obvious shot. However, she knows what she is doing and is strategically trying to put her team in a better position to score.

Marozsán is well loved by her teammates for her rather offbeat and quirky personality. She is particularly fond of singing to her teammates at various points during matches to perk them up. And her celebratory dance moves after scoring goals have become one of her trademarks.

*Henry has played for the French national team since her debut in 2009.*

# AMANDINE HENRY

Before Amandine Henry started playing midfield for the French women's national team, few people paid much attention to the team. While the women were always competing at a substantial level and even brought home some championships, it wasn't until the dazzling Henry started playing for them that France began to be looked at with admiration.

Like many other European women players, Henry started soccer at a very young age. When she was five, she joined boy's teams and competed in their often rough-and-tumble games. As a result, she learned how to play tough and took those skills with her when she started playing with other girls at the age of thirteen.

*Henry returned for a second stint with Lyon in 2018.*

## ON THE ROAD TO LYON

While Lyon was already the most successful team in France before Henry joined, she helped take them to a new level when she came on board. Before that, she started her career in 2004 at FCF Hénin-Beaumont at the age of fifteen. After one season there, she went to the women's section of the Clairefontaine Academy to work on her skills for two seasons.

As a result, she was able to join Lyon at age eighteen in 2007. Unfortunately, she tore cartilage in her knee during her first season and very nearly quit the sport altogether. However, she stuck around and got even better and helped lead Lyon to the UEFA Women's Championship in 2010, 2011, and 2012. But the talk of her skills got even louder after the 2015 FIFA Women's World Cup.

## WINNING THE SILVER BALL AWARD

The 2015 Women's World Cup was a particularly exciting event. While the same few teams flirted with claiming the title (with the United States eventually winning), France was a surprise contender that shocked a lot of people. And a lot of that had to do with Henry.

While she put only one ball in the back of the net during a 5–0 trouncing of Mexico, she still earned the Silver Ball Award as the second-best player of the tournament. She was then named one of the best players in Europe in 2015 when she was a finalist for the annual UEFA Best Women's Player in Europe Award. A large part of this had to do with her defensive ability.

As a midfielder, Henry is skilled at both offensive and defensive maneuvers. However, her signature is stopping an opponent's offensive play dead in its tracks and either getting the steal or redirecting play. That said, she is no slacker when it comes to scoring. Over her club career she has averaged a goal roughly every third match, which is strong for a defensively focused player. For France she plays a much more defensive role and therefore is not counted on to score often.

In her native France, Henry is hugely popular not only for her excellent on-field skills but also for her charismatic personality. She is particularly fond of making fun of her sometimes imperfect English during interviews and is known for cooking all of her meals at home—with the help of a robot partner!

# Text-Dependent Questions:

1. How old was Dzsenifer Marozsán when she started her professional career?

2. Who scored a hat trick against Japan in 2015 to help her team win the World Cup?

3. How many goals did Vivianne Miedema score in the 2015 World Cup qualifying games?

# Research Project:

Investigate the diets of the average female soccer player before a tournament, and create a list of the most common foods. Prepare a typical menu that represents this diet for an entire week.

 WORDS TO UNDERSTAND

**acumen**
keenness and depth of perception

**cap**
the term used to describe how many international matches
a player has appeared in

**clutch**
a tight or critical situation

**daunting**
seeming overwhelming to deal with in anticipation;
intimidating

**stifling**
making (something) difficult or impossible

# CHAPTER 4

# Dynamite Defenders

High-level soccer is primarily a defensive game. Teams tend to focus much more on strategies that prevent opponents from scoring rather than on scoring goals themselves. In order to succeed, teams must be sound at the back. Good defenders are essential for good teams.

# KADEISHA BUCHANAN

When it comes to center backs and defenders, few have captured the imagination of their home countries or the world quite like Kadeisha Buchanan. This defender has been a member of the Canadian national team since she was seventeen, debuting January 12, 2013. And just two years later, at the age of nineteen, she won the Young Player Award at the 2015 Women's World Cup.

This early introduction to the national team was probably no surprise for those who coached her in the Canadian youth soccer program. Starting when she was just fourteen years old in 2010, she quickly improved her skills and won a silver medal at the 2012 CONCACAF Women's U-17 Championship. Her strong defensive skills and physical playing style made her one of the key defensive players in the entire tournament.

# THE IMPORTANCE OF DEFENSE IN SOCCER

The general public often overlooks a defender like Buchanan. Many fans are looking for those dazzling goals and exciting dribbles past opponents. As a result, it is harder for some people to assess the impact defenders have on the game. That's because there are very few statistics to track their success, and few defenders score goals at the same rate as forwards or even midfielders.

However, the many awards Buchanan has won over the years highlight the importance of defense in soccer and her contributions to her teams. For example, while playing at the University of West Virginia in 2015 she was a finalist for the Missouri Athletic Club's Hermann Trophy, one of the most respected trophies in all of female soccer. Later in 2016, she won the Hardman Award, an award that goes to West Virginia's top amateur athletes. She was the first woman to win this award since Olympic gold-medal-winning gymnast Mary Lou Retton in 1984.

*Buchanan won the Hardman Award while at West Virginia University in 2016, becoming the first female winner since 1984.*

# GOING PROFESSIONAL

In 2016, Buchanan signed her first pro deal with Lyon in France and helped lead them to Division 1 Féminine and Coupe de France championships in the 2016–2017 season. In the same season, Lyon won the UEFA Women's Championship League, anchored by her great defense. On the international scene, she helped Canada win a bronze medal in the 2016 Summer Olympics and led them to a win in the 2015 Four Nations Tournament.

# TOUGH DEFENSIVE PLAYS

While Buchanan is no stranger to scoring plays, her real value comes in her **stifling** defense. With fast feet, an innate understanding of the flow of soccer games, and a willingness to get tough, Buchanan is skilled at getting into position to disrupt her opponent's scoring attempts. She is also willing to fight for the ball and get it out of dangerous territory.

*Buchanan looks on as two players battle for the ball during a match between Canada and Australia at the 2016 Olympic Games.*

Positioning is everything when it comes to soccer defense, a fact that can be hard for many casual fans to understand. The science of soccer defense comes easily to Buchanan, which makes her a constant threat to her opponents. Getting past her requires a willingness either to take a chance on a one-on-one dribble and risk a steal or to attempt a risky pass.

In spite of her obvious skills and impact on the game, Buchanan is known to be rather soft-spoken and humble. A big part of that is due to her upbringing, as she was the youngest of seven sisters raised by a single mom in a household where hard work and focus were expectations.

 ## Inspirational Quotes

Soccer is filled with a large number of inspirational quotes from players that showcase how important this sport is for its fans and the athletes who love it. For example, player Abby Wambach had this to say about the game and its impact on young girls: "We need to have women in more powerful positions that are making decisions, so when that ten-year-old girl is looking up and wondering, 'What can I do and what do I want to be when I get older?', she has the opportunity to do and be whatever she wants." This quote indicates how seriously these professionals take their sport. In other parts of the world outside of the United States, opportunities for girls are even fewer, so hearing words of encouragement from the sport's leaders is a big deal.

# NILLA FISCHER

Many of today's most promising defenders are young, like Kadeisha Buchanan, and have their best years ahead of them. Sweden's Nilla Fischer is one of the older players on this list but appears to still have many great years of soccer ahead of her. While she is in her mid-thirties, her skills as a defender haven't dipped in the slightest and may even be getting better.

Fischer serves as an inspiration to players who face the challenge of switching positions, as a 2013 change to center back after a career as a defensive midfielder has showcased her impressive soccer IQ. In fact, it shows that her skills had been undervalued for most of her career.

In addition, she served as an inspiration to LGBTQ athletes everywhere when she married her female partner in 2013. Fischer is a strong advocate for gender equality in soccer and has been particularly prominent in promoting LGBTQ rights. During a match against Bayern Munich in 2017, she wore a rainbow armband to show her support, in spite of death threats against her from offended fans and residents of Germany.

*Fischer, seen here receiving an embrace from a teammate, has been thrilled with her move from midfield to defender for Sweden.*

# INTERNATIONAL PLAY

Unlike some of the younger players at the 2019 FIFA Women's World Cup, Fischer is a seasoned pro at international competition. She has already played on three Women's World Cup teams, including leading the 2011 team to a third-place showing. And her Olympic experience is just as storied. In 2008 and 2012, Sweden moved on to the quarterfinals before being eliminated. They went on to pick up a silver medal in 2016.

While Sweden has yet to win an international championship, they remain a **daunting** team who is likely to give opponents a significant challenge. For example, in the 2016 Summer Olympics they were the first team to score a goal. And which player was it that put the ball into the back of the net? It was Fischer, celebrating her switch to center back with an offensive contribution.

## MAKING A POSITIONAL SWITCH

Ever since 2001, Fischer had excelled at a defensive midfielder position. As she was approaching one hundred **caps** for Sweden, her coach Pia Sundhage decided that Fischer was being underutilized. As a result, she switched her to a center back position in 2013. It was a move that paid off right away.

For example, she scored three goals in the UEFA Women's Euro 2013 Championship and helped her team move on to the semifinals. At that point, she was offered a contract from VfL Wolfsburg based on her performance in those matches. She agreed to join the team and has been there ever since. With this club, she won the UEFA Women's Champions League in the 2013–2014 season, the Frauen-Bundesliga title in 2013–2014 and 2016–2017, and the DFB-Pokal (German Cup) for three straight seasons starting in 2014–2015.

*Watch Fischer discuss the tough defense of the Swedish team.*

# DEFENSE PAYS OFF FOR FISCHER

Though Fischer has scored her fair share of goals over the years, she remains a defensive player at heart. In fact, she won the Silver Boot for the 2013 UEFA Women's European Championship, Best Swedish Female Defender in 2013 and 2014, and was third place in the UEFA Best Women's Player in Europe Award in 2014. All of these awards coincided with her switch to center back.

This position seems to suit Fischer's style of tough and aggressive soccer. She is not content to watch her opponents develop plays but instead continually looks for ways to throw them off or disrupt their flow. Beyond that, she is a skilled dribbler and passer, making her a dual threat when it comes time to move forward or shut down an opponent's offensive drive.

*Fischer (center) sports the gold medal Sweden won at the 2016 Olympic games at a celebration for the team in Stockholm.*

# STEPH HOUGHTON

When English women's soccer fans think of high-quality defenders, they probably imagine Steph Houghton. This player has been competing at a high level for most of her career and has shown both defensive excellence and offensive skills. Her greatest moment likely came in the 2012 London Olympics. In spite of being a defender, Houghton scored three of England's goals in their four games. In fact, she scored the winning goals against New Zealand and Brazil to push England into a fifth-place finish.

That kind of **clutch** play is nothing new from Houghton. It's part of why she's earned more than eighty caps for the England national team and why she was made the captain of the English team in 2014. And like Fischer, Houghton is a diverse player. In fact, she started her career as an offensively dominant striker before being moved to midfield and defensive positions later in her career.

*Houghton [R] won the FA WSL title with Arsenal in 2011.*

Though many female soccer players balk at being labeled role models, Houghton revels in it. She wants to inspire more girls to take up the sport and advance it to higher levels of success. To reach that goal, she has become one of the friendliest and most approachable players in the sport, regularly taking selfies with dedicated fans.

# WHERE HER SUCCESS BEGAN

Houghton started her career with the junior and senior teams of the Sunderland AFC Ladies, which played at the time in a third-tier women's league. She peaked with this team when she helped them win promotion to the National Premier Division in 2005–2006. Her skills helped her win Football Association (FA) Young Player of the Year in 2006–2007 and made her a highly sought-after player that season. Arsenal and Everton were particularly interested in her after this successful showing, but Leeds United Ladies successfully recruited her after Sunderland was demoted from the Premier Division.

Houghton helped Leeds win the 2010 FA Women's Premiere League Cup and then moved on to Arsenal in the following season. Later on, she joined Manchester City FC in 2014. Like Fischer, Houghton works primarily as a center back. Her position here is unusual because she started her career as an offensive player. However, her intelligence on defense has only grown since she made the switch, which has made her one of the most devastating two-way players in the world.

# SUCCESS IN THE WORLD CUP

There have been only a few disappointments in Houghton's career. The first and worst was likely when she missed the 2007 FIFA Women's World Cup with a broken leg. She then later missed Euro 2009 with a damaged knee ligament. The 2013 last-place finish in the UEFA Women's Euro was another heart-breaking moment for her. However, those disappointments were wiped clean after the 2015 World Cup.

During this event, she was team captain (since 2014) and scored her first World Cup goal in the round of sixteen against Norway. Her steady defensive presence helped England earn its first semifinals appearance of all time. And with four more years under her belt as a player, Houghton is likely sgunning for an even better showing in 2019.

# SECRET SCORING WEAPON

Defenders are rarely considered real scoring threats in soccer, but Houghton might be the exception to that idea. With Leeds United Ladies, she scored nine goals in forty-five appearances between 2007 and 2010.

And with Arsenal Ladies from 2010 to 2013, she scored eleven goals in seventy-four appearances. And since her 2014 switch to Manchester City, she has put seven in the back of the net through the 2017–2018 season.

That's twenty-seven goals just for her club teams. On the national team, she has scored fourteen goals through the 2017 season. This gives her a total of forty-one goals since 2007, which is

*Houghton has worn the captain's armband for England since 2014.*

not a bad rate for a defender. One of her best goals came in a match for Arsenal against Lincoln. From at least fifty yards back, she powered the ball into the net for a dazzling and perfectly placed shot. It's those kinds of moments that make Houghton such a thrilling player to watch and one that might just surprise many in the 2019 FIFA Women's World Cup.

# BECKY SAUERBRUNN

The skill of the United States women's soccer team has been apparent since the beginning of the Women's World Cup in 1991. They not only won that inaugural event but also have won two other championships and have never placed lower than third. One reason for their success is the development of young players like Becky Sauerbrunn.

Sauerbrunn is a veteran contributor to the national soccer team and has been appearing with them since 2008. During her decade-long career on this team, she has become one of the most reliable and capable defenders in the world. Her skills and dedication are likely to translate to another strong showing from the U.S. women's soccer team in 2019.

As a leader, Sauerbrunn doesn't scream at her teammates or shame them. To her, that kind of behavior is cruel and unnecessary. Instead, she prefers to lead by example by excelling in the sport at the highest level. In this way, she's become one of the most respected leaders of the U.S. National Team.

# EARLY DEDICATION

A big reason for Sauerbrunn's success over the years is her early dedication to the sport. Her first significant opportunity was to attend the U-14 Girl's National Team Identification Program. During this event, her skills were noticed and worked on by professionals. As a result, she was skilled enough to join the U-16 Women's National Team in 2000 and continued to play with them for two years.

During this time, she appeared on a U-16 team at the United States Amateur Soccer Festival. She was part of the team

*Sauerbrunn has been co-captain for the USWNT since 2016.*

that pulled off a 5–1 win against a Region IV team and later helped her squad draw the final match 2–2 against the USASA National Select Team. This early success expanded through play with various squads until the day she was first called up for the USWNT.

*Sauerbrunn took time to grow into her role with the USWNT. She did not become a regular starter until she had been with the team for five years.*

# INTERNATIONAL COMPETITION

Sauerbrunn's continued success in youth leagues is what drew the attention of the USWNT. It called her up in 2008 and featured her in a six-day training camp. This event climaxed with her being named to the Four Nations Tournament in China. Even though she scored a goal against Canada during that tournament, she was not called back to the national team until 2010.

In 2010, training camp was held in Atlanta to determine the team for the 2010 CONCACAF Women's World Cup Qualifying Tournament. While Sauerbrunn's appearances there were limited, the team did qualify for the 2011 FIFA Women's World Cup, and Sauerbrunn was chosen for the team as a defender. Most of her experience at this event was in practice and training, as she took part in multiple training camps leading up to the World Cup. Ultimately, Sauerbrunn played only in the semifinal game against France and helped her team win 3–1.

When the 2012 Summer Olympics rolled around, she was named to the Women's Olympic Qualifying Team. They won the qualification tournament to snatch a spot in the competition. After several tough matches leading up to the Olympics, Sauerbrunn was chosen as one of the eighteen players to represent America, playing thirty-eight minutes across three games and winning a gold medal in the process.

# BECOMING A CONSISTENT STARTER

During her early days on the national team, Sauerbrunn was mostly on the sidelines. However, her skills had improved enough by 2013 that she was regularly starting in most matches. And by the time the 2015 Women's World Cup came around, she was the only player on the U.S. team to start all twenty-five matches leading up to the tournament and played 2,184 minutes—the most of any player on the team.

Her increased playing time came on the back of her increasingly intelligent defensive play. She is known as an on-field general whose acumen is without peer. She was a significant part of the 2015 World Cup 5–2 win over Japan, as she and the backfield continually shut down Japan's fast-paced defense and kept them from making any comebacks. Sauerbrunn was named co-captain along with Carli Lloyd in 2016.

## Text-Dependent Questions:

1. How old was Kadeisha Buchanan when she won the Coupe de France Championship for the 2016–2017 season?

2. How many minutes did Becky Sauerbrunn play in 2015?

3. Which player helped England win its first semifinals appearance in the 2015 World Cup?

## Research Project:

Research the average training routine of a female soccer player and attempt one of their workouts. Don't hesitate to take a break if it is too challenging for you to handle at first. Write down your thoughts about the routine and how tough it would be to do every day.

 WORDS TO UNDERSTAND

**gregarious**
fond of company; sociable

**meticulous**
showing great attention to detail; very careful and precise

**top flight**
the highest or most outstanding level, as in achievement or development

**transcendent**
beyond or above the range of normal or merely physical human experience

**waive**
to release a player from a team

# CHAPTER 5

# The Keepers

At soccer's highest level, a match between two evenly skilled sides will feature very few good opportunities to score. Even the world's best defenses cannot keep the top players in the world in check for an entire match, however. That is when the goalkeeper is expected to shine. Being in the right position and reacting without hesitation are essential goalie qualities when the opposing striker finds the ball and a clear shooting lane. In a sport where a single goal means so much, having a great goalkeeper means even more.

# HEDVIG LINDAHL

When it comes to goalkeepers around the world, few are as **transcendent** as Sweden's Hedvig Lindahl at her best. This player started her career at a young age and was impressive almost immediately. For example, she was awarded a rare five stars when selected for the 1998 All-Star Team at the prestigious Elite Girls Camp in Halmstad. Lindahl was the only player at the camp that season to receive this high score.

Due to her skills and the lack of available girl's teams at the time, she started her junior career at age four with Gropptorps IF, which was a boy's team. Seven years on this team helped prepare her for the challenge of heavy-duty female competition later in her career.

Lindahl has stated that one of her primary goals as a player is to bring more attention to the rights of LGBTQ citizens around the world. She and her wife have two children together and volunteer for various groups as a way of raising awareness of the challenges faced by LGBTQ individuals in soccer and elsewhere.

# EARLY CLUB LEAGUE SUCCESS

Four years into her senior career, Lindahl was scouted by Malmö FF Dam, a top team in the Damallsvenskan, the top women's league in Sweden. She signed with Malmö in 2001 as the backup to national team goalkeeper,

*Lindahl has received high marks for her goalkeeping skills since making an impression at a prestigious soccer camp at age 15.*

Caroline Jonsson, who taught her a lot about playing the position. With Malmö already having an established goalkeeper with Jonsson, Lindahl got sent to Linköpings FC for five seasons before joining with IFK Göteborg for two seasons.

While at IFK Göteborg, Lindahl was a dominating goalkeeper for the team. She recorded twenty-one shutouts in the forty-three matches she started. That's a nearly 50 percent rate, much higher than an average goalkeeper. However, Lindahl was shocked when her coach Torbjörn Nilsson refused to renew her contract. This action forced her to join Kristianstads DFF for the 2011 season.

She has since moved on to join Chelsea in England's top league and is currently their starting goalkeeper. One of her biggest triumphs during this time was during the 2015 FA Women's Cup Final, in which she forced a shutout of Notts County to get the win. Later in the same year, she stunned Sunderland with a 4–0 blanking and earned the club's first FA Women's Super League (WSL) Title.

# SUCCESS IN THE WORLD CUP

During the 2007 FIFA Women's World Cup, national team coach Thomas Dennerby chose Lindahl as the team's starting keeper. In spite of coming in second the previous tournament, Sweden did not make it out of the group stage, and Lindahl was bitterly disappointed. In the following year's summer Olympics, they made it to the quarterfinals but ended up ranked eighth, another disappointment for the team.

However, Lindahl was retained by Dennerby for the 2011 Women's World Cup in Germany and did not let her team down. With her skilled presence between the posts, she helped Sweden secure a third-place finish, their second best of all time. And while the 2012 Olympics had a similar result as the 2008 games, the 2016 team finished with a silver medal. Unfortunately, the 2015 World Cup team slipped out of the tournament at the round of sixteen, with a record of 0–3–1.

In spite of that unfortunately early exit, Lindahl still had a good performance against Germany in a 4–1 loss. Even though she gave up four goals, she did make several tough saves and helped keep her team in the lopsided game longer than expected. As a reward for her play, she was given the 2015 Diamantbollen, which is the award for the best female player in Sweden.

# SARI VAN VEENENDAAL

Anyone who watches British women's soccer has probably seen Sari van Veenendaal in the net for Arsenal. And if they have seen her play, they know that this Dutch player is one of the top players in the world. In fact, there are some who are predicting that Van Veenendaal could be the key ingredient that the Netherlands needs to make a real dent at the 2019 FIFA Women's World Cup.

The Dutch team certainly has a lot to prove this year. After two decades of failing to qualify for the World Cup final tournament, they finally made it in for the 2015 event. And while they were eliminated in the round of sixteen, they came in a respectable thirteen of twenty-four teams. And with van Veenendaal making her first appearance between the posts in this tournament, this humble Dutch team suddenly looks very promising.

## SUCCESS COMES QUICKLY

At the tender age of seventeen, van Veendendaal was chosen to play for club team FC Utrecht. She was primarily there as an understudy to Angela Christ. During that time, Christ taught van Veenendaal a variety of techniques and helped her improve her hand and foot speed. As a result, van Veendendaal was ready to move on to FC Twente in 2010 and to begin her career as a starting goalkeeper. In her debut season she won the Eredivisie, which is the highest level of professional football in the Netherlands. She also picked up BeNe League titles in 2013, 2014, and 2015.

After winning that last BeNe League title, she joined top English club Arsenal and helped lead the team to the 2015 FA WSL Cup. And in 2016, she was one of the primary architects of a 2016 FA Women's Cup victory. The final game was a real nail-biter and put Van Veenendaal under a lot of strain. She did not buckle, but rather blanked Chelsea in a 1–0 win.

*Van Veenendaal has been the starting goalkeeper for Arsenal since 2015.*

# WORLD STAGE

Van Veenendaal did not abandon her Dutch team either, but helped propel them to their first European Championship in 2017. During this tournament, she started in all six games and allowed just three goals. After this successful and unprecedented run for the team, Prime Minister Mark Rutte and Minister of Sports Edith Schippers made them Knights of the Order of Orange-Nassau, which is a Dutch order of chivalry. The order has been in operation since 1892 and honors those who are deemed to have earned special honors for the country. Receiving this award is one of the biggest honors Dutch citizens can receive.

# MODERN GOALKEEPING STYLE

Van Veenendaal brings a modern style of play to the sport. Keepers in the Netherlands utilize what has become known as the Dutch style, which starts from the back near the net and plays outward.

This approach gives keepers more reaction time when compared to the more conservative front approach.

As a result, van Veenendaal and Arsenal have had an increasing amount of success over the last few seasons. The most recent is an FA WSL Cup title in the 2017-2018 season. With her fast hands, quick feet, and **top-flight** reflexes, Van Veenendaal may help the Netherlands improve their standing in the 2019 FIFA Women's World Cup.

*Check out these astonishing saves by Sari van Veenendaal.*

In spite of her obvious success, van Veenendaal consistently talks about improving her skills as a player. During an interview after being named as Arsenal's number-one goalkeeper, she said, "I think I can still develop myself, and I'm feeling better every year. I've learned a lot here and have great teammates and staff around me. I think that will help me to develop myself every single week, every single day, to be the best Sari I can be."

# SARAH BOUHADDI

French-born goalkeeper Sarah Bouhaddi is in a unique position going into the 2019 FIFA Women's World Cup. As her team automatically qualifies for its first home-country World Cup, it hopes to make a big splash and to compete on a high level. This is particularly true because the team has failed to qualify in four of the eight Women's World Cup appearances since 1991, and in 2018 the men's team won the FIFA World Cup, intensifying the spotlight on France.

The women's French squad has been competitive since qualifying for the 2011 tournament, after not qualifying in 2007. In 2011 France had its highest ranking ever with a fourth-place finish. And in 2015, it finished fifth and made it to the quarterfinals. After years of failing to qualify for the Olympics, France finally did so in 2012 and 2016, coming in fourth in its first appearance.

# SARAH
# BOUHADDI

**FRANCE/LYON**

More Than **90** clean sheets in club play

**9**

Consecutive
Division 1
Féminine
League Titles
(2010-18)

**2X**

IFHHS World's
Best Woman
Goalkeeper
(2016, 2017)

**5**

UEFA Women's Champions League Titles (2011, 2012, 2016, 2017, 2018)

**6**

Consecutive Coupe de France Féminine National Championships (2012-17)

More Than

**100**

Club Wins

More Than

**120**

Caps for France

Is it any coincidence that Bouhaddi played in three out of these four campaigns? Probably not, as she has become one of the most respected and well-known goalkeepers in the world. And after nearly making it to the final match two tournaments in a row, expect the French squad and Bouhaddi to come out swinging.

*Bouhaddi's addition to the French national team coincided with a reversal of fortune for the squad that had struggled to qualify for major tournaments.*

# FRANCE'S BEST GOALKEEPER

For years, Bouhaddi has been known as the best goalkeeper in France. Even after suffering a torn ACL in 2011 and taking time off to recover, she was still good enough to get on the 2012 Summer Olympic squad. All of this success started at a young age, as Bouhaddi led the U-19 French team to a 2003 UEFA Women's Under-19 Championship. Just seventeen years old, she was named the team's starting keeper. During this championship run she blanked both England and Norway.

Two years later, at just nineteen, she was chosen as the senior team starting goalkeeper for the UEFA Women's Euro 2005. In spite of its early elimination in the group stage, she was selected as the team's number- one goalkeeper for the 2007 FIFA Women's World Cup qualifying matches. Unfortunately, the team was unable to qualify that year.

That failure rested heavily on her shoulders, though it was a combined lack of scoring and defensive pressure that kept France out of the tournament. Starting in 2009 she played for Lyon and helped the team retain a dominance rarely seen in the sport. And though a knee injury (torn ACL) kept her out of the 2011 World Cup, she did participate in the 2015 tournament and provided a steady hand and skilled presence in the net.

# FAN FAVORITE

Thanks to her rather **gregarious** and outgoing personality, Bouhaddi has become a household name in much of France. The country is particularly proud of her for staying in France and playing with local favorite Lyon. But don't let her friendly personality throw you off when it comes to her competitive spirit. Once the whistle blows, Bouhaddi plays to win.

Expect to see her showing off some incredible diving saves and her sound play in the box whenever she steps on the pitch. Bouhaddi is known for her expert positioning during matches and her ability to read plays as they develop. She rarely gets caught following a trap and therefore lets few balls get past her. Perhaps that's why Lyon has won the Division 1 Féminine every year since 2009, the Coupe de France Féminine between 2011 and 2017, and the UEFA Women's Champions League five of the last eight years.

Bouhaddi is known to be a determined on-field general for her team. Between the posts, she can be heard shouting commands and play ideas to defenders while she sets up defense for free kicks. She is stoic after giving up a goal and avoids falling into a spiral of self-doubt that could cost her team the match. Instead, she waves it off and gets back into the game.

# LYDIA WILLIAMS

Many young goalkeepers are coming to the 2019 FIFA Women's World Cup with wide eyes and huge ambitions. Australian keeper Lydia Williams, however, has already been there three times, and was the starter in 2015. And while the team has yet to get out of the quarterfinals stage or finish higher than seventh, Williams and the Matildas have reason to expect better in 2019.

In 2016 Australia was one of just twelve teams to qualify for the 2016 Olympic games in Brazil, where it lost in the quarterfinals. Williams allowed just four goals in three matches, including one clean sheet. In 2018 FIFA had Australia ranked as a top-10 team in the world all year. Could the 2019 World Cup be the time that Australia leaps out of the quarterfinals and becomes a championship contender?

# INTERESTING AND INSPIRING

Williams grew up in the Kalgoorlie area of Western Australia, having been born to a father of Aboriginal descent who worked as a missionary. Her early career in soccer started when she joined the Australian Institute of Sport Football Program. In this program, she found that she excelled in the goal and enjoyed playing this position above all others. Her dedication to goalkeeping has been severely tested over the years as she suffered injuries that would end the careers of less dedicated players.

Williams' early life as the daughter of missionaries helped to shape her success as a keeper. Forced to continually move and make new friends and teammates, she developed an innate inner strength that keeps her strong even during tough matches. It also helped her become a leader on the field, in spite of a somewhat shy and introverted personality.

With practice and dedication, she was able to join the W-League team Canberra United in 2008. She stayed with this squad until 2014 when the Western New York Flash signed her. They tagged her as their starting goalkeeper and featured her in fourteen different games. Before tearing her ACL in the 2014 AFC Women's Asian Cup, she had recorded two shutouts.

*Williams took over as the starter in goal for Australia in 2012.*

Unfortunately, this injury started a tumultuous period that saw Williams get **waived** by both the Flash and then the Washington Spirit, who subsequently cut her before the start of the 2015 season. After a year of sustained recovery effort, she was signed by the Houston Dash and was then loaned to Melbourne City before being traded to Seattle Reign FC. By this point, she had finally fully overcome her ACL injury and was playing with the same level of skill she had in her early World Cup appearances.

# WILLIAMS NEVER GIVES UP IN THE GOAL

One of the keys to Williams' success is her **meticulous** approach to her position. She spends hours every day practicing, including taking shots at strange or awkward angles. Beyond this focus and dedication, she is known to have some of the fastest hands in the business and a wingspan that opponents struggle to shoot past.

Williams is going to have to be on top of her game throughout the 2019 FIFA Women's Word Cup. While Australia has solid players on its team capable of scoring and sustaining a defense, they have very few genuine superstars. As a result, Williams is going to be the bedrock on which they build their chances of championship success in 2019.

## Text-Dependent Questions:

1. Which goalkeeper won the 2015 Diamantbollen for being the best female player in Sweden?

2. Who brought the Dutch style to English goalkeeping?

3. Where did Lydia Williams start her professional career?

## Research Project:

Research women soccer players throughout history and create your own ultimate World Cup Dream Team. You can include inactive players or even those who have passed away. Include statistics explaining why you chose them and brief discussions of the role they would play in your soccer strategy.

**Club:** collective name for a team, and the organization that runs it.

**CONCACAF:** acronym for the *Confederation of North, Central American and Caribbean Association Football*, the governing body of the sport in North and Central America and the Caribbean; pronounced "kon-ka-kaff".

**Extra time:** additional period, normally two halves of 15 minutes, used to determine the winner in some tied cup matches.

**Full-time:** the end of the game, signaled by the referees whistle (also known as the *final whistle*).

**Goal difference:** net difference between goals scored and goals conceded. Used to differentiate league or group stage positions when clubs are tied on points.

**Hat trick:** when a player scores three goals in a single match.

**Own goal:** where a player scores a goal against her own team, usually as the result of an error.

**Penalty area:** rectangular area measuring 44 yards (40.2 meters) by 18 yards (16.5 meters) in front of each goal; commonly called "the box".

**Penalty kick:** kick taken 12 yards (11 meters) from goal, awarded when a team commits a foul inside its own penalty area.

**Penalty shootout:** method of deciding a match in a knockout competition, which has ended in a draw after full-time and extra-time. Players from each side take turns to attempt to score a penalty kick against the opposition goalkeeper. Sudden death is introduced if scores are level after each side has taken five penalties.

**Side:** Another word for team

**Stoppage time:** an additional number of minutes at the end of each half, determined by the match officials, to compensate for time lost during the game. Informally known by various names, including *injury time* and *added time*.

**UEFA:** acronym for *Union of European Football Associations*, the governing body of the sport in Europe; pronounced "you-eh-fa".

Englund, Tony. *Soccer Goalkeeper Training: The Comprehensive Guide.* Aldershot, England: Meyer & Meyer Sport, 2017.

Jordan, James. *It Pays to Win on Defense: A Game-Based Soccer Approach to Developing Highly Effective Defenders.* Independently Published: CreateSpace Independent Publishing Platform, 2015.

Lisi, Clemente A. *The U.S. Women's Soccer Team: An American Success Story.* Lanham, MD: Scarecrow Press, 2013.

Lloyd, Carli. *When Nobody Was Watching: My Hard-Fought Journey to the Top of the Soccer World.* Boston, MA: Mariner Book, September 5, 2017.

Morgan, Alex. *Breakaway: Beyond the Goal.* New York City, NY: Simon & Schuster Books for Young Readers, 2017.

# INTERNET RESOURCES

**https://www.fifa.com/womensworldcup/index.html**
The official FIFA news source for upcoming matches and tracking points and team placement during the tournament.

**https://www.ussoccer.com/womens-national-team#tab-1**
The official website for the United States Women's soccer team. This site includes news, videos, stories, and more.

**https://equalizersoccer.com/**
One of the leading independent magazines for news, features, and articles on women's soccer around the world.

**https://shekicks.net/**
Another online msagazine that focuses on a variety of tours and tournaments, mainly regional clubs.

**http://www.nwslsoccer.com/**
The official site of the NWSL soccer league, including updates on games, placings, and detailed player profiles.

# AUTHOR'S BIOGRAPHY

Bryce Kane is a professional writer with over ten years of experience. For three years, he worked as a sports writer for a daily newspaper covering a multitude of sporting events, including multiple state championships. In 2009, he earned a master's degree in fiction writing and is currently working on two books while enjoying a relaxing life in Traverse City, Michigan as a freelance writer.

# EDUCATIONAL VIDEO LINKS

**Chapter 1:** http://x-qr.net/1Dms

**Chapter 2:** http://x-qr.net/1EPx

**Chapter 3:** http://x-qr.net/1G7b

**Chapter 4:** http://x-qr.net/1H3r

**Chapter 5:** http://x-qr.net/1D8Q

# PICTURE CREDITS